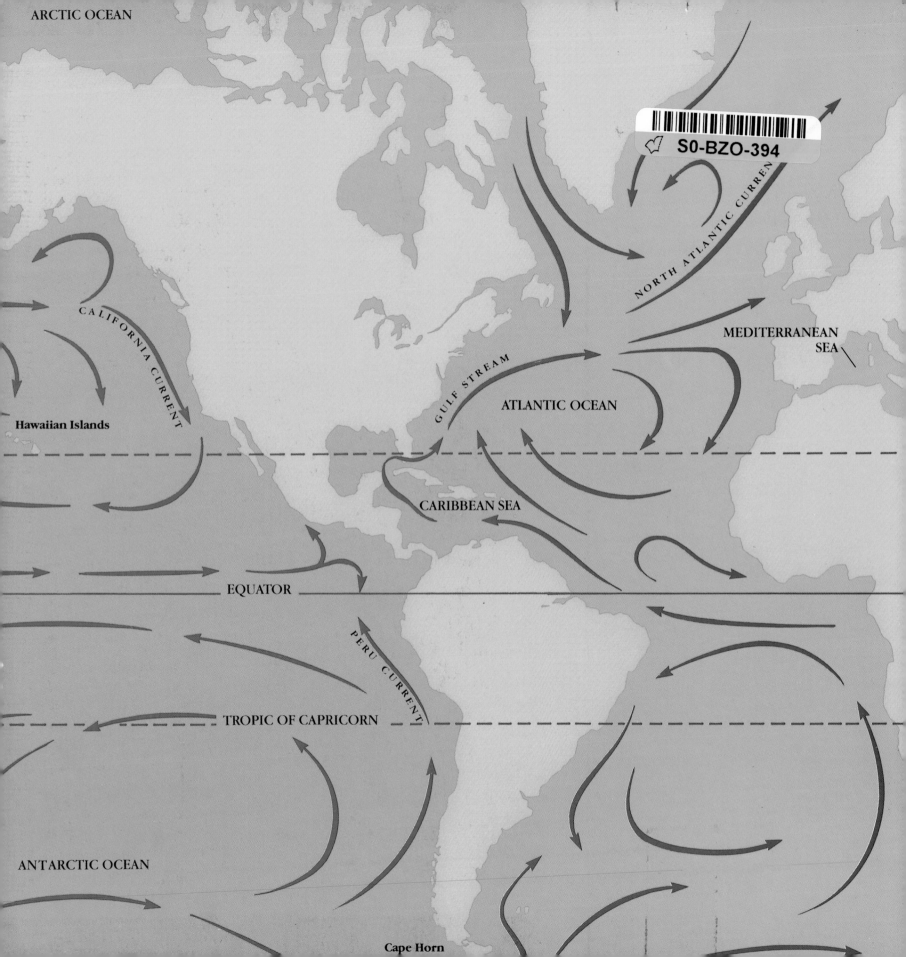

ARCTIC OCEAN

CALIFORNIA CURRENT

Hawaiian Islands

NORTH ATLANTIC CURRENT

MEDITERRANEAN SEA

GULF STREAM

ATLANTIC OCEAN

CARIBBEAN SEA

EQUATOR

PERU CURRENT

TROPIC OF CAPRICORN

ANTARCTIC OCEAN

Cape Horn

OCEANS

SEYMOUR SIMON

 Smithsonian | Collins

An Imprint of HarperCollinsPublishers

To Robert Simon and Nicole Fauteux

PHOTO AND ART CREDITS

Chuck Place: pages 26, 27, 29, 30, 32; Kimimasa Mayama/Corbis: page 19; NASA: pages 4, 7, 12, 13; NOAA: page 10; Nova Scotia Tourism Bureau: page 16; Terraphotographics/BPS: pages 21, 28, 31; United States Coast Guard: page 24; Woods Hole Oceanographic Institution: page 9 (by James Broda); endpapers and drawings on pages 14 and 15 and pages 22 and 23 by Frank Schwarz.

The name of the Smithsonian, Smithsonian Institution and the sunburst logo
are registered trademarks of the Smithsonian Institution.

Collins is an imprint of HarperCollins Publishers.

Library of Congress Cataloging-in-Publication Data
Simon, Seymour.
Oceans / Seymour Simon.
p. cm.
Summary: Text and photographs explore the physical characteristics, life forms, and fragility of the world's oceans.
ISBN-10: 0-06-088998-5 (trade bdg.) — ISBN-13: 978-0-06-088998-2 (trade bdg.)
ISBN-10: 0-06-088999-3 (pbk.) — ISBN-13: 978-0-06-088999-9 (pbk.)
1. Oceans—Juvenile literature. [1. Ocean.] I. Title.
GC21.5.S58 1990   89-28452
551.46—dc20   CIP
                                                                             AC
1 2 3 4 5 6 7 8 9 10
❖
Revised Edition

Smithsonian Mission Statement

For more than 160 years, the Smithsonian has remained true to its mission, "the increase and diffusion of knowledge." Today the Smithsonian is not only the world's largest provider of museum experiences supported by authoritative scholarship in science, history, and the arts but also an international leader in scientific research and exploration. The Smithsonian offers the world a picture of America, and America a picture of the world.

Earth is different from any other planet or moon in the Solar System: It is the only one with liquid water on its surface. In fact, more than 70 percent of the earth's surface is covered by oceans. Although we speak of the Atlantic and Pacific as separate oceans, the world is really covered by a single body of water in which the continents are islands.

Echo soundings of the ocean floor show mountains more than twice as tall as Mt. Everest and canyons six times as deep as the Grand Canyon. A computer was used to produce this map of the land beneath the waves. Blues show the deepest spots and yellows the shallowest; the average depth is two and a quarter miles.

The main features on the map are: the Mid-Atlantic Ridge (1), part of the longest mountain chain in the world; deep-ocean trenches (2, 3); and undersea mountains that rise above the waves to become islands (4, 5).

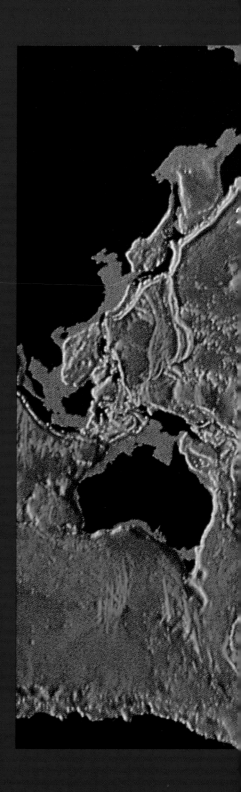

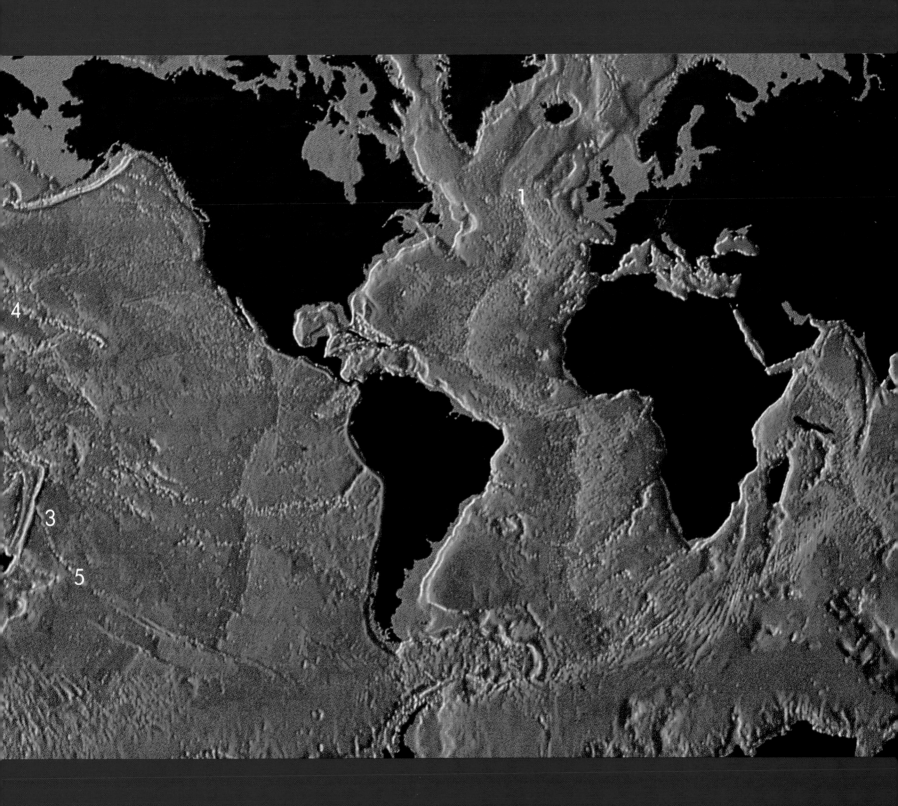

There is an enormous amount of water in the oceans, more than one-and-one-half quintillion (15 followed by 17 zeros) tons. That's 100 billion gallons for each person in the world. Yet the amount of water in the oceans has remained much the same for many millions of years. That is because most of the water that evaporates into the air returns to the sea in the form of rain or snow. Even the water that falls on land finally runs downhill in rivers and streams to the sea.

All this water is constantly in motion, driven by the sun's energy. The sun warms ocean waters, especially in the tropics, where the sun's rays are more direct. That warms the air at the surface of the waters, which then picks up moisture. Some of the moisture in the air condenses into clouds, releasing more heat into the atmosphere. The uneven heating causes winds that blow across the surface of the sea, producing waves and currents. These carry heat energy for thousands of miles from the warm waters around the equator to the colder waters of the polar regions.

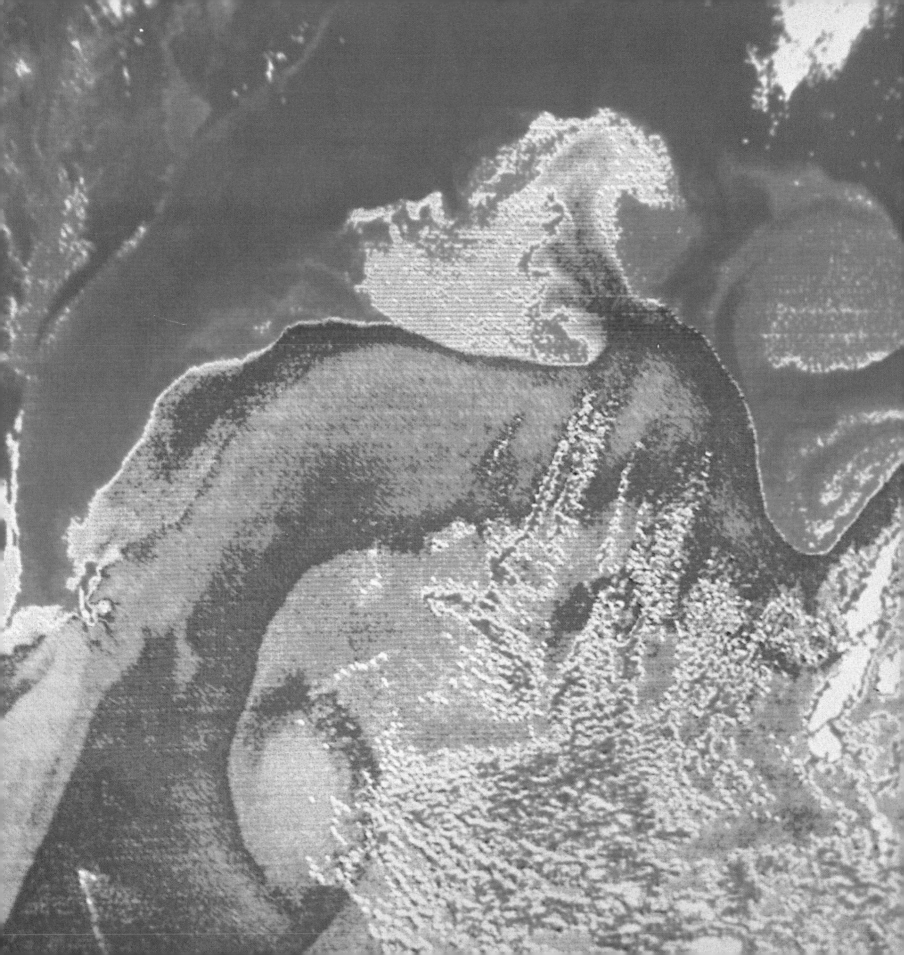

The major ocean currents of the world flow in huge circular paths called gyres. This satellite photo shows a section of the warm Gulf Stream, part of the North Atlantic Gyre. The computer-generated colors show water temperatures from the warmest (red) to the coolest (blue). The Gulf Stream swirls up the east coast of North America and out into the Atlantic at a speed of up to one hundred miles a day. In the middle of the Atlantic, the Gulf Stream divides, and part of it becomes the North Atlantic Current. This flows past Northern Europe, making the climate warmer and milder than it might be otherwise. In the Pacific, the warm Japan Current becomes the North Pacific Current and then moderates the climate on the west coast of the United States and Canada.

Sometimes, the normal pattern of ocean currents changes and the results can be a disaster. One of the world's major fisheries is in the cool, nutrient-rich waters off the coast of Peru. Every few years, however, the cool water warms and the sea life disappears. This strange change is known as El Niño. These computer-generated maps show what happens: The blues are the coldest waters; reds, the warmest waters. The image on the left shows the warm currents (1) that produce normal weather in most years. The green area (2) shows the cool waters usually found off the coast of Peru. The

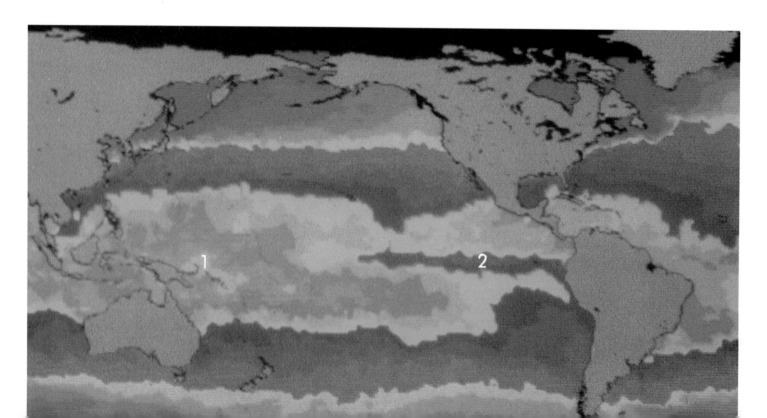

image on the right shows that during El Niño, the warm currents have cooled (4) and the cool waters have warmed (3).

During the winter of 1997–1998 the biggest El Niño of the century was under way, and all around the Pacific, climates changed. Australia suffered one of the worst droughts in two hundred years, causing immense dust storms and fires. On the west coast of South America, heavy rains up to three times above normal flooded the region, and in the United States, record snow fell in the Rocky Mountains, which resulted in heavy flooding in the spring.

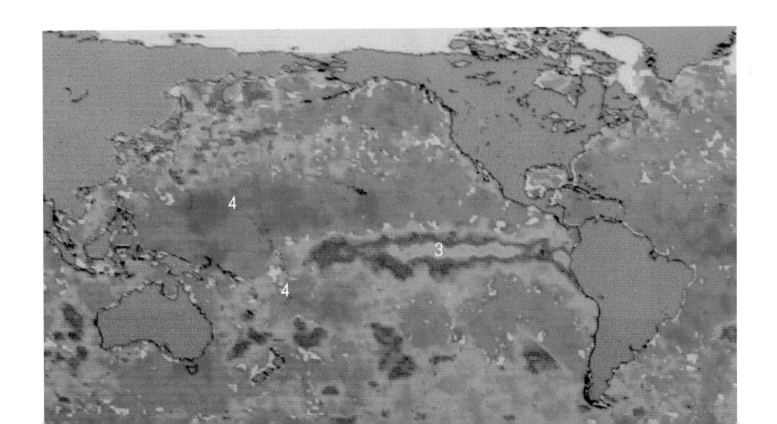

If you visit the shore, you'll soon notice the daily rise and fall of the water, which we call tides. Tides are caused by the gravitational pull of the moon and the sun. Even though the moon is much smaller than the sun, the moon is so much closer to the earth that its pull is much stronger. As the earth rotates, the ocean waters nearest the moon are pulled outward in a traveling bulge called high tide. There is also a traveling tidal bulge on the side of the earth opposite the moon. Here, the moon's pull on the waters is less, so there is a second high tide. Because of the double tidal bulges, most places on the coast have two high and two low tides every twenty-four hours and fifty minutes.

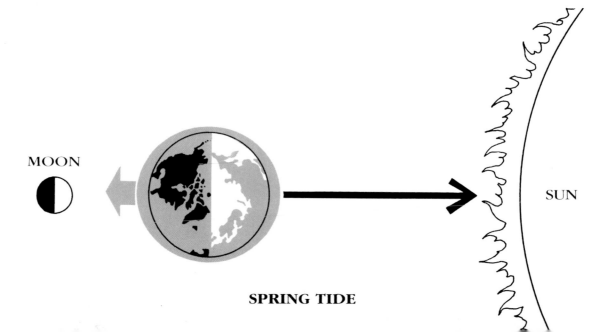

MOON

SUN

SPRING TIDE

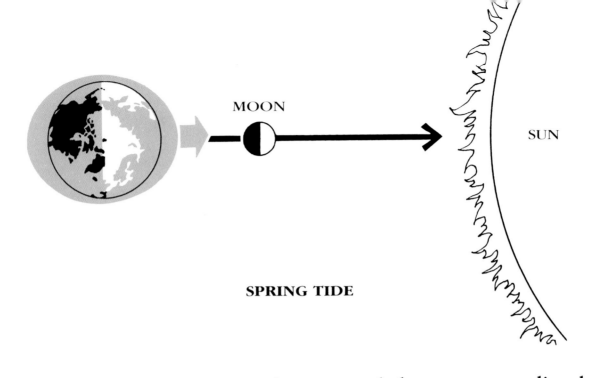

SPRING TIDE

Twice a month, when the sun and the moon are lined up with the earth, their gravitational pulls combine and produce the biggest tides, called spring tides. The sun and moon also pull at right angles to each other twice a month. Then we get the smallest tides, called neap tides.

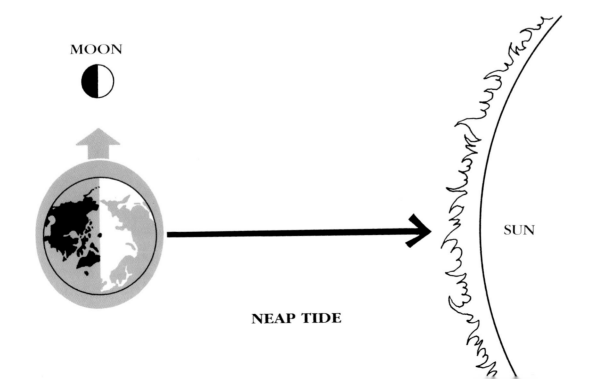

NEAP TIDE

Even in places close together, tides do not always occur at the same time or have the same size. The time and size of the tides depend upon the shape of the shore and the width of the gulfs and bays. Think of an ocean as a kind of large, shallow pan of water sloshing back and forth. The water in the middle of the ocean moves up and down very little. The water at each end of the ocean moves up and down much more. Because of this, islands in the middle of the ocean, such as Hawaii, often have small tides compared to the lands around the edges of an ocean.

If a tide can spread out, such as in the wide Gulf of Mexico, it may rise and fall only a few inches a day. When the tide cannot spread out, the tides are much greater. The photos show an inlet in the narrow Bay of Fundy in Nova Scotia, where high tide may be fifty feet higher than low tide.

The waves commonly called tidal waves really have no connection with the daily tides. The name scientists use for this kind of wave is tsunami, pronounced SUE-nami, a Japanese word for sea wave. A tsunami is generated by a violent undersea earthquake or volcanic explosion. The shock forms a wave that can move across an ocean at 500 miles per hour, as fast as a jet plane. In the open ocean, a tsunami is only two or three feet high and hardly noticeable; but when it approaches a shore, a tsunami may build up to a huge size and hit with the force of a runaway train.

On December 26, 2004, a tsunami battered the island of Sumatra in Indonesia. The photograph shows the city of Banda Aceh still flooded a month later. The underwater earthquake that triggered the Sumatra tsunami created the longest fault rupture ever recorded. The rupture in the seafloor is nearly 800 miles long, and the earth is ripped apart by as much as 50 feet in places.

When the wind blows across the surface of ocean waters, little ripples form. As the wind continues to blow, the ripples grow into waves. The size of a wave depends upon the speed of the wind, how long it blows, and the fetch. The fetch is the distance over which the wave travels. The faster the wind, the longer it blows, and the greater the fetch, the bigger the waves.

In the open ocean, where the wind is blowing and making waves, the waves are all different sizes and shapes and go in different directions. As the waves move away from where they began, some travel faster than others and they form groups of about the same wavelength. The waves are now long and smooth and are called a swell.

WAVE ENERGY

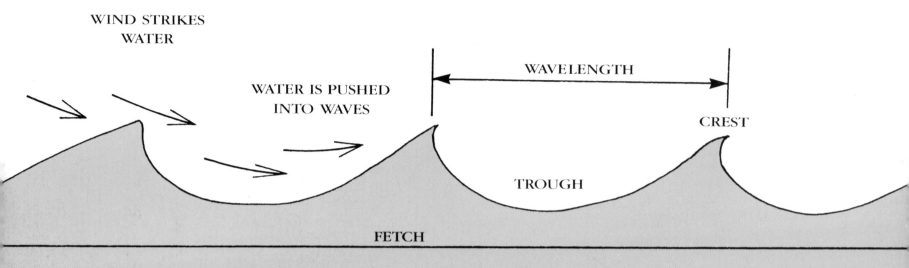

WIND STRIKES
WATER

WATER IS PUSHED
INTO WAVES

WAVELENGTH

CREST

TROUGH

FETCH

Waves moving across the ocean carry the energy of the wind, but the ocean water does not move along with the wave. As the wave passes, the particles of water move up and down and around in a little circle. If you watch a stick floating on water as waves pass by, you'll see that it bobs up and down but stays in just about

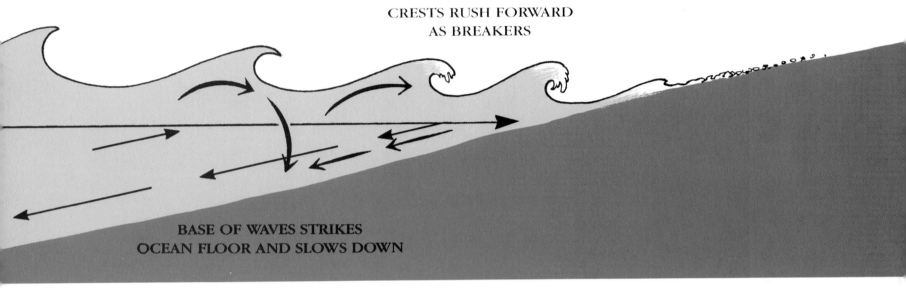

CRESTS RUSH FORWARD
AS BREAKERS

BASE OF WAVES STRIKES
OCEAN FLOOR AND SLOWS DOWN

the same place. Only the energy of the waves moves forward.

The high spot of a wave is called a crest and the low spot is called a trough. The distance between two crests (or two troughs) is called the wavelength. The height of a wave is the distance from crest to trough.

Storm-driven waves in the ocean can build up to great heights. One of the largest waves ever was 112 feet high, the height of a ten-story building. Oceangoing ships can ride over most waves. Small ships can ride up one side of a wave and down the other. Large ships can usually ride through waves without too much difficulty. During a hurricane or severe storm, however, a huge wave can dump hundreds of tons of water onto a ship in a few seconds, smashing it apart and sending it to the bottom.

When an ocean wave reaches the shallow water of shore, it begins to travel more slowly and its shape begins to change. Some people say that "the wave begins to feel the bottom." Waves begin to pile up and grow higher as those in the back come in faster than those in the front are moving.

As the waves slow down, the crest of the wave tries to continue at the same speed, until finally it topples over into the trough of the wave in front and becomes a breaker.

When waves break on the shore, the surf begins. Sometimes surf can break just a few yards from shore. However, if the shore is shallow, surf can form hundreds of yards out to sea. The waves on shallow beaches, such as this one in Hawaii, spill over slowly as they roll up the shore.

Even rocky coastlines are worn away by the power of the surf. The softer kinds of rock are worn away first, leaving rocky spires or platforms of harder rock. These, too, will eventually be worn down by the pounding of the waves. In other places, the incoming surf carries sand particles from one spot to another, slowly building up beaches and dunes. Every moment of every day, the sea is at work reshaping the land.

Millions upon millions of years ago, life began in the sea. Today, the sea is home to incredible numbers of living things, from microscopic plants and animals called plankton to giant whales larger than any dinosaur. Some animals are drifters, others swim freely, and still others spend their entire lives on the bottom of the sea.

One way or another, all sea animals depend upon the multitudes of tiny plankton plants, which drift in the surface waters of the ocean, using the energy of sunlight to produce food. The tiny plants are eaten by small fish and other animals, which are eaten by large animals, and which are eaten, in turn, by even larger animals. Many tons of sea animals of all kinds are eaten each day by people all over the world.

Throughout the ages, the sea has been the inspiration for art, music, and poetry, as well as a source of food and a highway to travel. The sea has also been used as the world's wastebasket for garbage and even radio-active wastes. Until now, the sea has always been able to renew itself, but we are reaching the limits of this vast ocean world. And without the sea, the earth would be a world without life.

JAPAN CURRENT

TROPIC OF CANCER

PACIFIC OCEAN

EQUATOR

INDIAN OCEAN

TROPIC OF CAPRICORN

Cape of
Good Hope